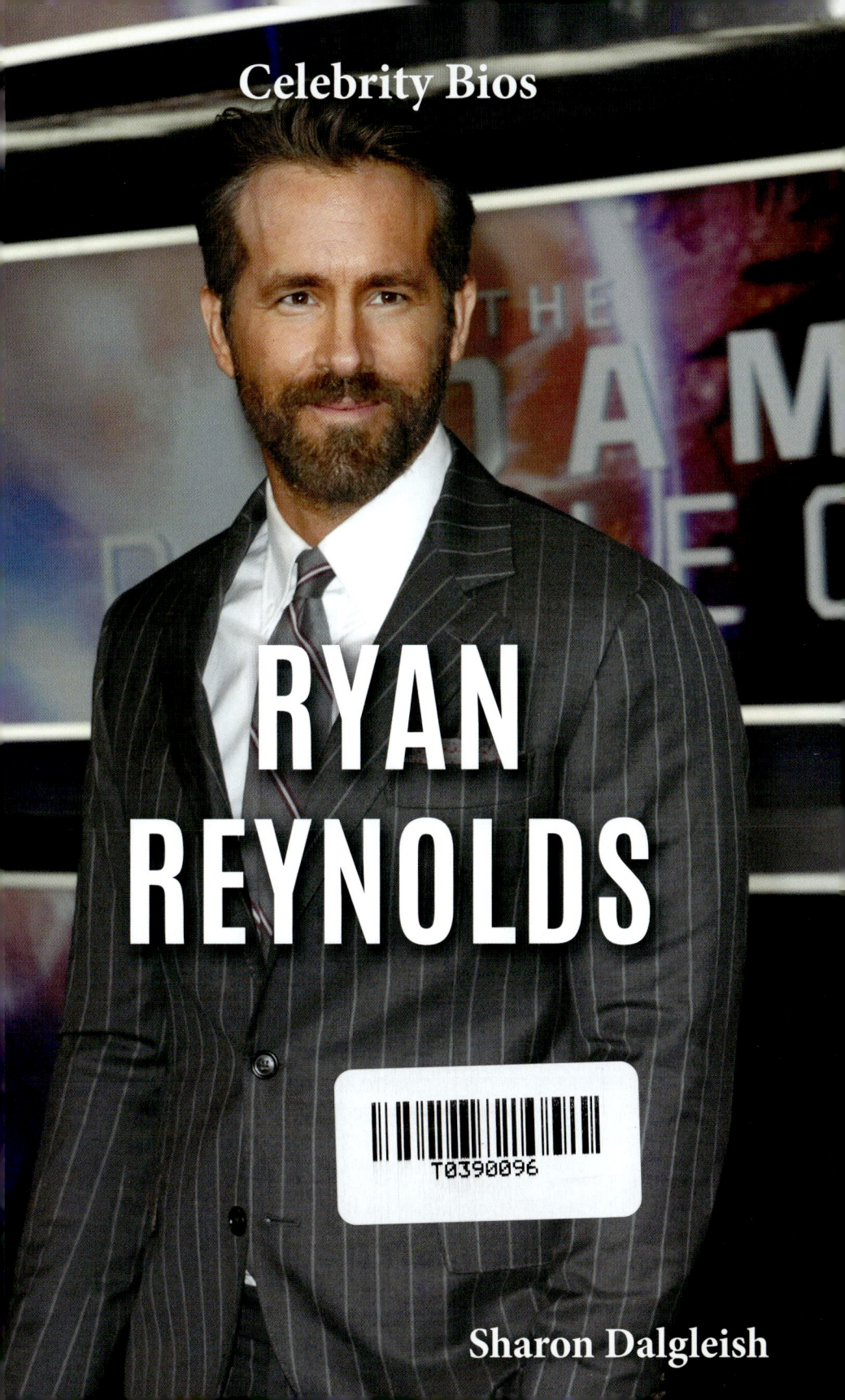

Celebrity Bios

RYAN REYNOLDS

Sharon Dalgleish

Apex is distributed by North Star Editions:
sales@northstareditions.com | 888-417-0195

Produced for Apex by Red Line Editorial.

Photographs ©: John Nacion/Star Max/IPx/AP Images, cover, 1; Marvel Enterprises/Album/Alamy, 4–5; Chiang Ying-ying/AP Images, 6–7; Shutterstock Images, 8–9, 10–11, 12–13, 14–15, 16–17, 20–21, 26–27, 28–29, 32–33, 38–39, 42–43, 44–45, 56–57, 58; Jeff Kravitz/FilmMagic, Inc/Getty Images, 18–19, 40–41; Ron Galella/Ron Galella Collection/Getty Images, 22–23, 24–25; Pictorial Press Ltd/Alamy, 30–31; Charles Sykes/Invision/AP Images, 34–35, 52–53; Chris Pizzello/Invision/AP Images, 37; Evan Agostini/Invision/AP Images, 46–47; Arturo Holmes/WireImage/Getty Images, 49; Sthanlee B. Mirador/Sipa USA/AP Images, 50–51; Martin Rickett/EMPPL PA Wire/AP Images, 54–55

Library of Congress Control Number: 2023924696

ISBN
979-8-89250-219-1 (hardcover)
979-8-89250-240-5 (paperback)
979-8-89250-280-1 (ebook pdf)
979-8-89250-261-0 (hosted ebook)

Printed in the United States of America
Mankato, MN
082024

NOTE TO PARENTS AND EDUCATORS

Apex books are designed to build literacy skills in striving readers. Exciting, high-interest content attracts and holds readers' attention. The text is carefully leveled to allow students to achieve success quickly.

TABLE OF CONTENTS

Chapter 1

BECOMING DEADPOOL

It's 2015. Ryan Reynolds walks into the costume workshop for the movie *Deadpool*. The Deadpool suit waits under a spotlight. The designers worked hard on it. Now, he finally sees the finished suit. It looks just like the one in the comic books. He is so happy that tears run down his cheeks.

Designers wanted Deadpool's suit to look used and lived-in.

Reynolds puts the costume on. But there is one problem. It doesn't fit. Helpers take out the suit's extra padding. Reynolds doesn't need the fake muscles. He tries the suit on again. This time, it fits perfectly. Reynolds is ready to play the antihero.

A KEEPSAKE

After filming the first *Deadpool* movie, Reynolds took the suit home with him. He wore it trick-or-treating. After that, he kept it in his basement.

Ryan Reynolds loves the character Deadpool. He has played the antihero several times.

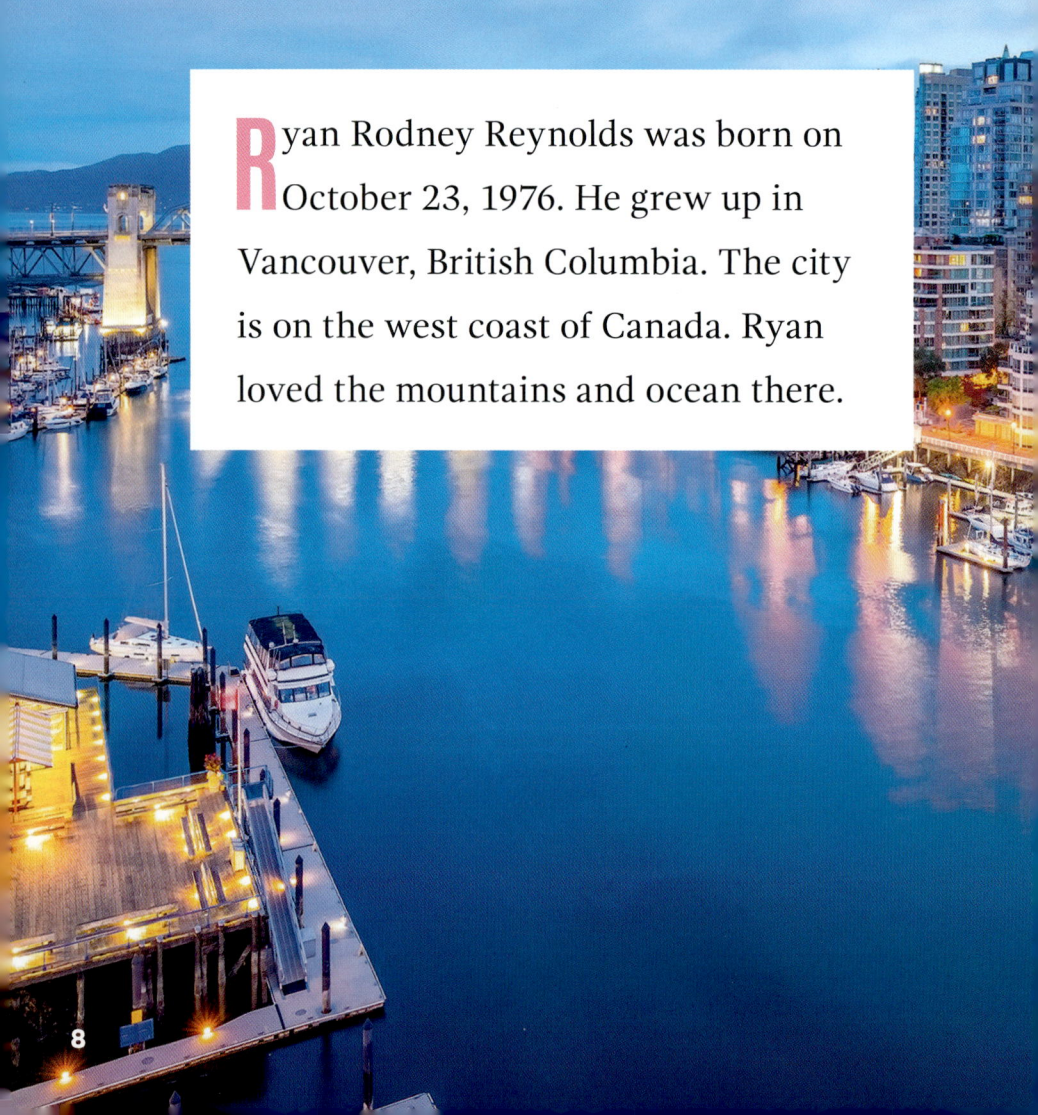

Chapter 2

EARLY LIFE

Ryan Rodney Reynolds was born on October 23, 1976. He grew up in Vancouver, British Columbia. The city is on the west coast of Canada. Ryan loved the mountains and ocean there.

Many movies and TV shows are filmed in Vancouver.

Ryan's dad had worked as a police officer. He could be strict and angry. Ryan was often stressed at home. He worked hard not to make his dad upset. As a kid, Ryan played sports. He also took drama classes. He especially loved doing improv. Improv let him be free and wild.

MAKING IT UP

In improv, there is no script. Actors make up the words as they go. They make up the story. They often create the characters and settings, too. Doing improv can help actors gain experience. It helps them listen and react to what others say or do.

Many actors performed in improv crews before they got famous.

When Ryan was 13, TV producers were making a show called *Fifteen*. They wanted people to audition. They asked schools to send their best drama students. Ryan had failed his drama class. He wasn't sent to the casting call. But he went anyway. Ryan got the role of Billy. He went to Florida to film the show. He appeared in 18 episodes.

At casting calls, many actors come to try out for a role.

CASTING →

HILLSIDE

Fifteen aired in the United States. It also aired in Canada. In Canada, the show had a different name. It was called *Hillside*. Kids in the show went to Hillside School.

The Canadian Broadcasting Corporation (CBC) makes many TV shows in Canada, including *The Odyssey*.

After filming *Fifteen*, Ryan went back to Vancouver. He worked on finishing high school. But Ryan also kept acting. He made his own improv group called Yellow Snow. In 1993, he appeared in *The Odyssey*. It was a fantasy TV show. The main character went to another world. Ryan played Macro. That character wanted to become powerful.

FAMILY PHOTOS

Ryan's father loved taking photos. He took hundreds at every family event. At first, this annoyed Ryan. But he got used to posing for photos. That was useful for acting jobs.

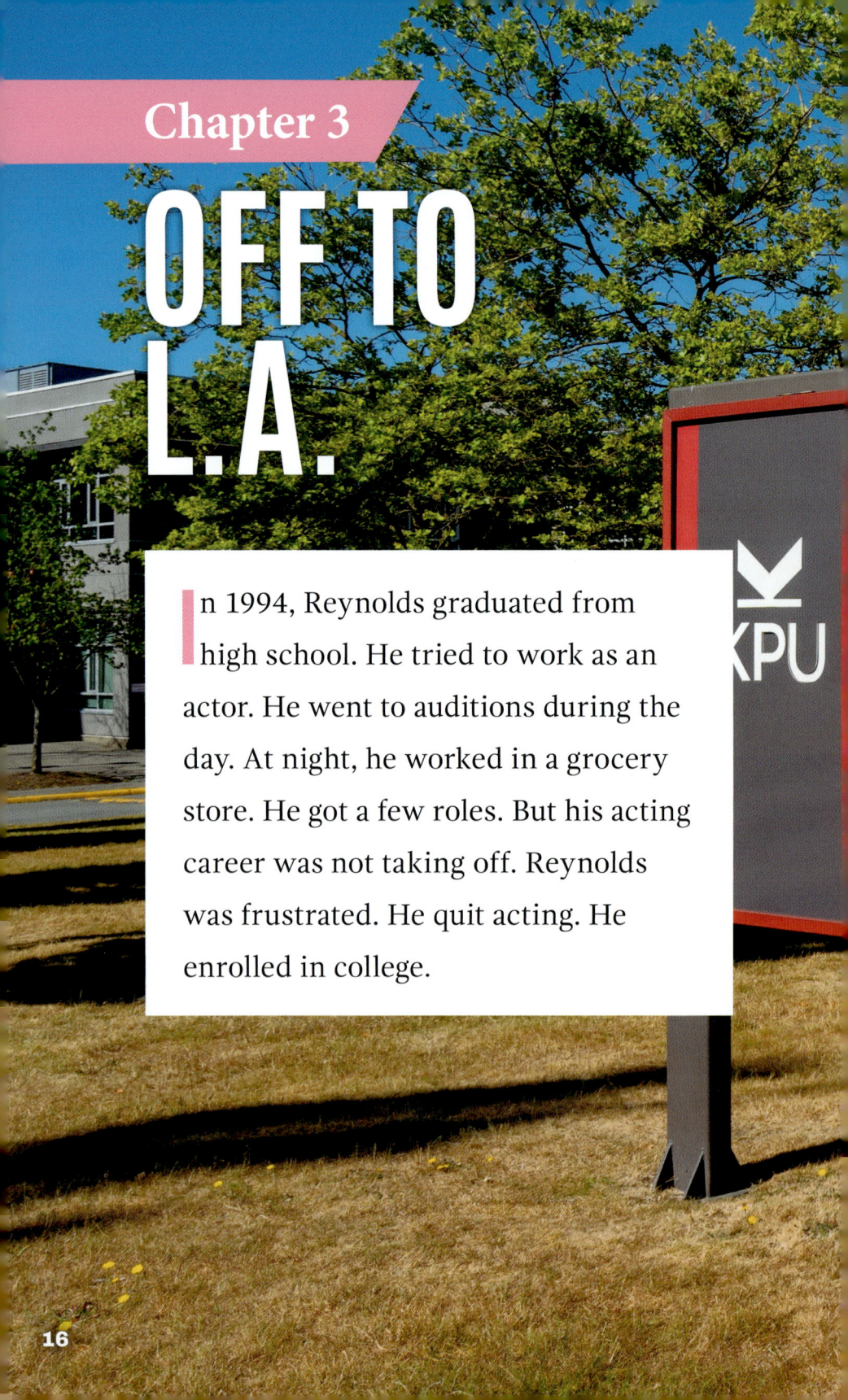

Chapter 3

OFF TO L.A.

In 1994, Reynolds graduated from high school. He tried to work as an actor. He went to auditions during the day. At night, he worked in a grocery store. He got a few roles. But his acting career was not taking off. Reynolds was frustrated. He quit acting. He enrolled in college.

Reynolds went to Kwantlen Polytechnic University. The school is south of Vancouver.

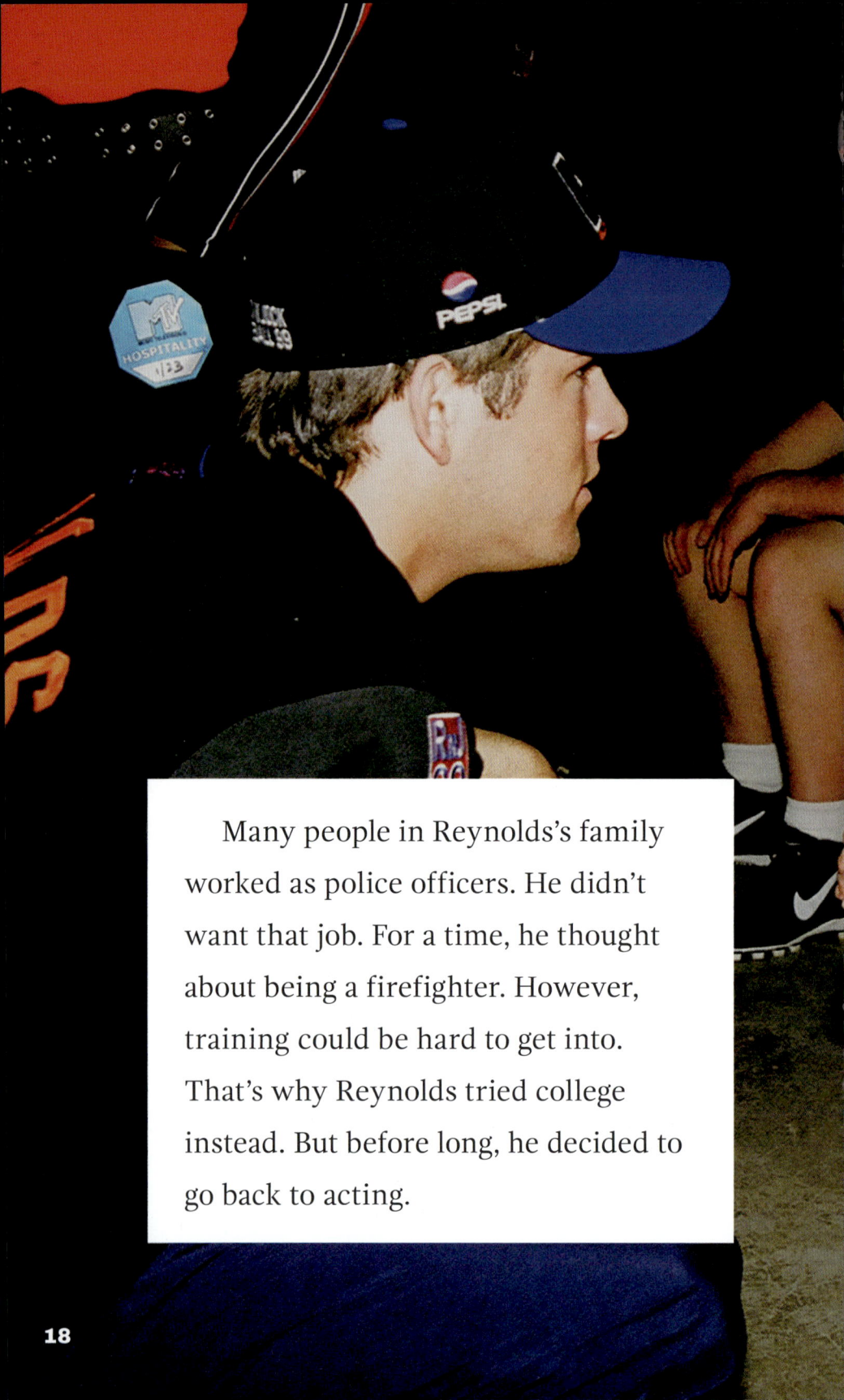

Many people in Reynolds's family worked as police officers. He didn't want that job. For a time, he thought about being a firefighter. However, training could be hard to get into. That's why Reynolds tried college instead. But before long, he decided to go back to acting.

A NEW CHANCE

In 1996, Reynolds landed a role in a TV movie. It was *Sabrina the Teenage Witch*. Reynolds played Seth. He was the school heartthrob.

Melissa Joan Hart (right) played the lead in *Sabrina*. She and Reynolds became friends.

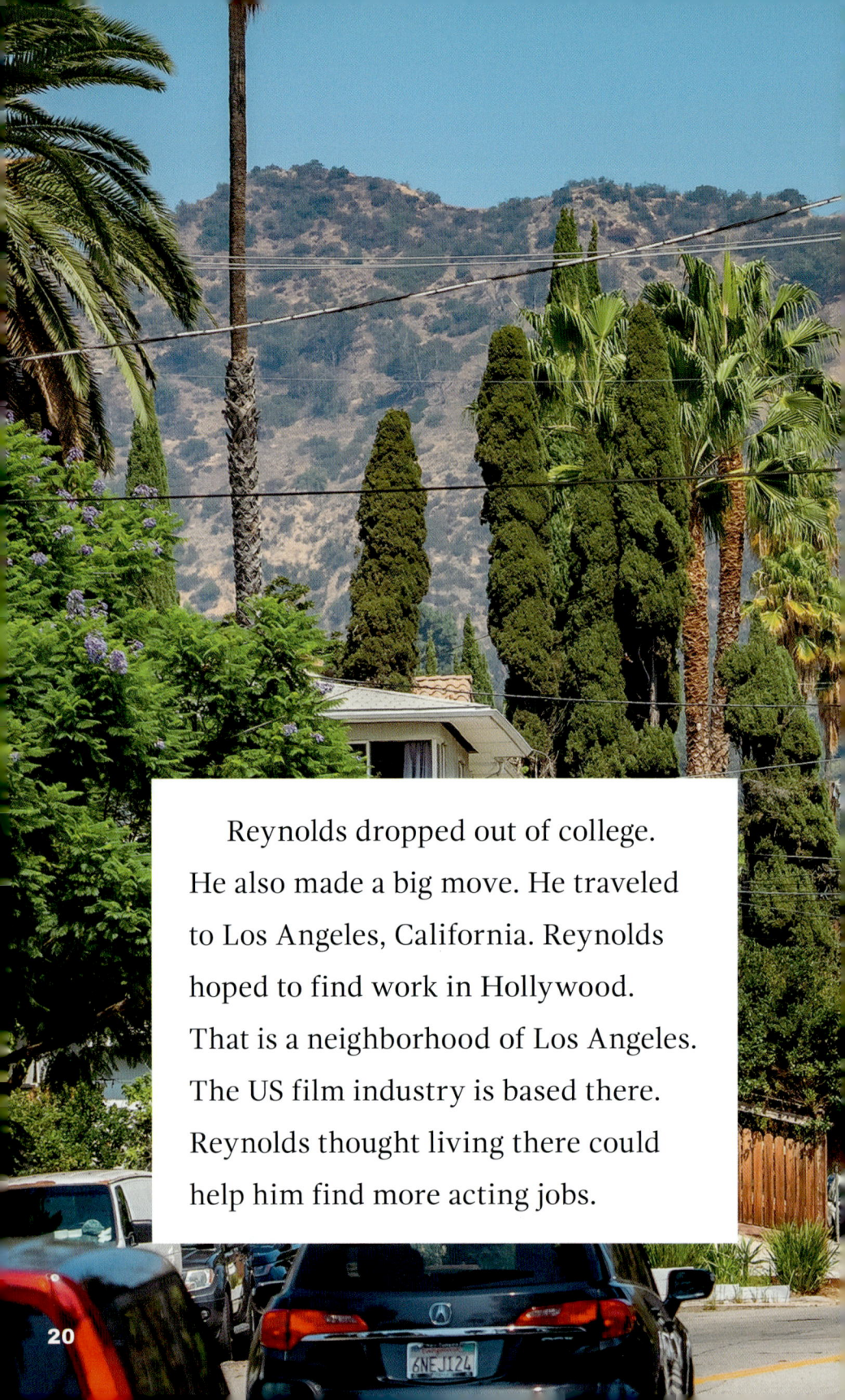

Reynolds dropped out of college. He also made a big move. He traveled to Los Angeles, California. Reynolds hoped to find work in Hollywood. That is a neighborhood of Los Angeles. The US film industry is based there. Reynolds thought living there could help him find more acting jobs.

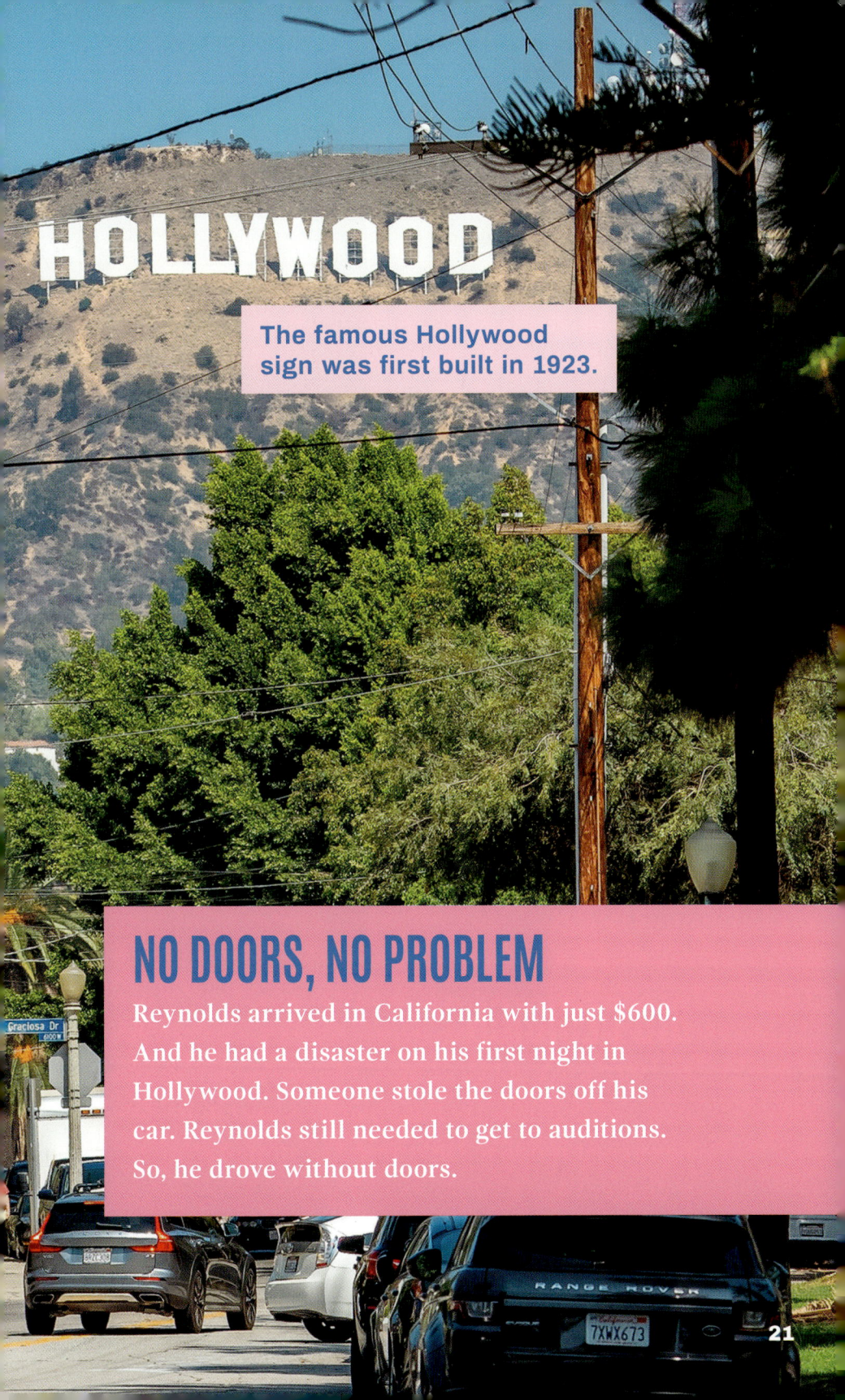

The famous Hollywood sign was first built in 1923.

NO DOORS, NO PROBLEM

Reynolds arrived in California with just $600. And he had a disaster on his first night in Hollywood. Someone stole the doors off his car. Reynolds still needed to get to auditions. So, he drove without doors.

After moving, Reynolds found a few small parts in films and TV shows. Then, in 1997, he landed a lead role in a sitcom. The show was called *Two Guys, a Girl, and a Pizza Place*. It was about three friends. Reynolds played one of them. The two guys were roommates. They worked in a pizza place. The third friend lived upstairs.

BIG DECISIONS

In 1997, Reynolds was offered a big role. It was Xander in *Buffy the Vampire Slayer*. But he turned it down. He wanted to stop playing teenagers.

Traylor Howard (right) played Sharon. She lived upstairs from Reynolds's character.

23

Two Guys, a Girl, and a Pizza Place aired from 1998 to 2001. Reynolds (left) played a goofy character.

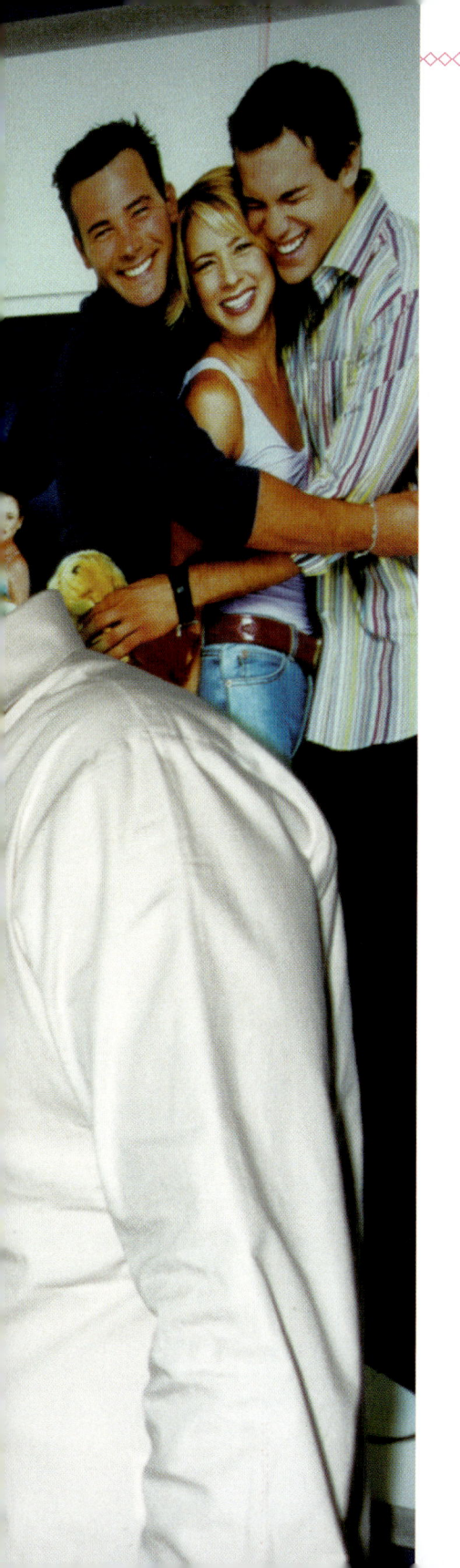

Reynolds played Berg. He was the smart-aleck friend. At first, some critics did not like the show. It did not have many viewers. But the show lasted four years. Berg was a breakout role for Reynolds. People noticed his natural skills for comedy.

Chapter 4

DIFFERENT ROLES

Reynolds had appeared in some small movies. But his first major film came out in 2002. *National Lampoon's Van Wilder* was a funny college movie. It became a big hit. Reynolds started earning more movie roles. He acted in funny movies, dramas, and action movies.

Reynolds was nominated for an MTV Movie Award for *Van Wilder.*

Audiences liked Reynolds's chemistry with Sandra Bullock in *The Proposal*.

In 2004, Reynolds starred in *Blade: Trinity.* It was an action film. In 2008, he starred in *Definitely, Maybe.* Then, in 2009, he acted in *The Proposal* with Sandra Bullock. Both movies were romcoms. They helped Reynolds become an even bigger star. Audiences liked his good looks and charm.

NOT SO SMOOTH

Reynolds was not always successful at dating. When he was 11, he liked a girl on the school bus. He tried to give her a cool look. He stepped off the bus. But he took too long. The bus doors closed on his backpack.

Reynolds became known as a hard worker. He continued landing movie roles. One was for the 2010 film *Buried*. Reynolds's character wakes up inside a coffin. He stays in it for the whole movie. Reynolds was afraid of tight spaces. But he overcame this fear for the role.

FACING FEARS

When Reynolds was 19, he went skydiving. His first parachute didn't open. He pulled the reserve chute and landed safely. But the accident scared him. He didn't like heights. In 2010, he had to film scenes while hanging by a wire. Doing that helped him face his fear.

In *Buried*, Reynolds's character must try to escape using a few items found in his coffin.

In *Green Lantern*, Blake Lively (left) played Hal Jordan's love interest.

In 2011, Reynolds played Hal Jordan in *Green Lantern*. It was his first lead role in a superhero movie. The movie was a flop. Some people said it had the worst superhero costume ever. Others said the story was poorly written. Others did not like the special effects.

WEDDING BELLS

Something good happened on *Green Lantern*'s set. Reynolds met his future wife. Blake Lively was his co-star. They began dating in 2011. They married in 2012.

In *Turbo*, Reynolds stars as a snail who tries to win the Indianapolis 500.

Reynolds also did voice acting for two animated movies. Both came out in 2013. *The Croods* was about a family of cavepeople. Reynolds was the voice of Guy. Guy lost his family. But then he met the Croods. *Turbo* was his other project. The film was about a garden snail. He dreamed of racing. Reynolds voiced the snail.

COMIC DREAMS

In 2004, Reynolds did not know who Deadpool was. But someone saw him in *Blade: Trinity*. They thought Reynolds could play Deadpool. So, they sent him a *Deadpool* comic book. Reynolds flipped it open. He saw his name in the comic. It said Deadpool looked like Reynolds crossed with a shar-pei dog.

Reynolds became a fan of the comics. He liked how clever and creative they were. For example, Deadpool talks to readers. He knows he's in a comic. And he makes lots of pop culture references.

Reynolds talks about Deadpool at San Diego Comic-Con in 2018.

Ryan Reynolds

Chapter 5

HAVING FUN

In 2016, Reynold starred as another superhero. This time, he played Deadpool. Reynolds had played the character once before. It was for *X-Men Origins: Wolverine* in 2009. Deadpool was just a small part of that movie. He didn't talk at all.

Hugh Jackman (right) played Wolverine in several different movies.

Reynolds won an MTV Movie Award for Best Comedic Actor for *Deadpool*.

In the comics, Deadpool is famous for making jokes. Reynolds wanted to make a funny Deadpool movie. He wanted Deadpool to be the main character. For years, Reynolds couldn't get a film studio to agree. Finally, Fox agreed. *Deadpool* was released in 2016. It was a smash hit. It broke box-office records. Critics and audiences loved it.

THE SECRET IS OUT

To help pitch his movie, Reynolds had test footage made. In 2014, someone leaked part of it. Fans loved it. The good response helped get the movie made.

Deadpool became a series. Reynolds co-wrote and starred in *Deadpool 2*. It came out in 2018. Then *Deadpool & Wolverine* came out in 2024. All three movies were full of jokes. They made fun of other Reynolds movies, too.

WRITING TIME

Reynolds has co-written many movies. He enjoys writing. He thinks it is hard to begin. He doesn't like looking at the blank screen. But he loves the work.

Fans often dress as Deadpool at comic book and gaming conventions.

The *Deadpool* movies are for adults. But Reynolds wanted to be in a movie his kids could watch. Soon, the chance came. The director for *Pokémon: Detective Pikachu* liked Reynolds. He thought the actor was good at funny improv. So, he hired Reynolds as Pikachu. In 2019, they recorded Reynolds's voice. They recorded his movements, too.

MANY JOBS

In 2021, Reynolds made the movie *Free Guy*. He starred in it. He also helped the writers with ideas. He helped produce it, too. *Free Guy* is about a background character in a video game. He becomes a hero.

Billboards in Times Square promoted the *Pikachu* movie.

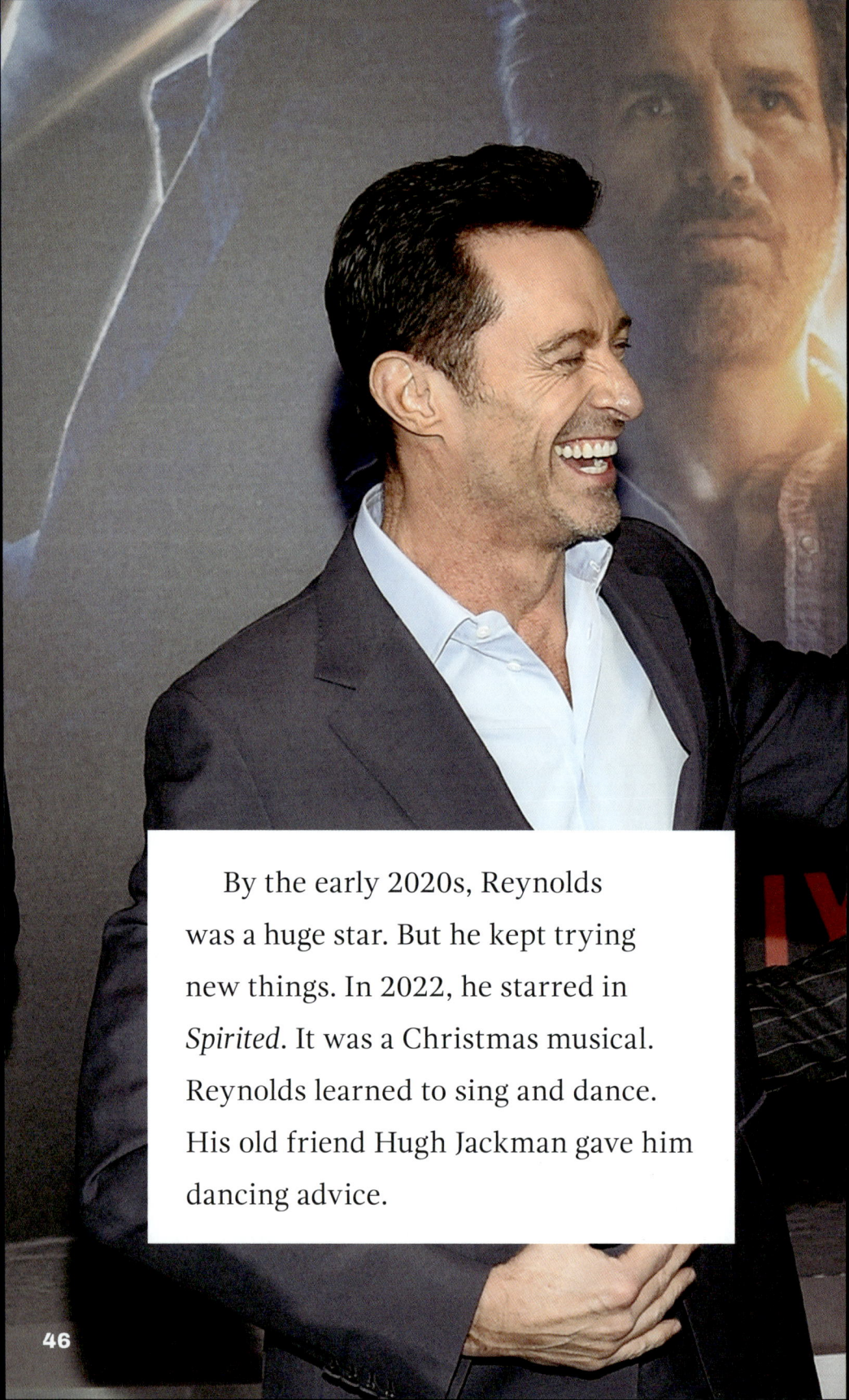

By the early 2020s, Reynolds was a huge star. But he kept trying new things. In 2022, he starred in *Spirited*. It was a Christmas musical. Reynolds learned to sing and dance. His old friend Hugh Jackman gave him dancing advice.

Reynolds and Hugh Jackman (left) became friends while making *X-Men Origins: Wolverine*. They often help promote each other's work.

CHRISTMAS CLASSIC

Spirited is loosely based on a book. That book is *A Christmas Carol* by Charles Dickens. Dickens wrote it in 1843. Many movies have been based on it.

MAXIMUM EFFORT

In 2018, Reynolds created a company. He called it Maximum Effort. That is something Deadpool says. Deadpool likes causing fun trouble. So does Reynolds. He wanted his company to be fun.

Maximum Effort makes ads. The ads tell stories. Many of them get millions of views on YouTube. The company makes movies, too. It made *Free Guy* in 2021. In 2023, the company made *Bedtime Stories with Ryan*.

Reynolds made short, funny videos to promote his film *Free Guy*.

Chapter 6

ICONIC ACTOR

In the 2020s, Reynolds was one of the highest-paid actors. He had tried acting, writing, and producing. But he was best known for funny roles. In 2022, he won a People's Choice Award. The award named him as an icon. He won an award for adding to the film industry, too.

Reynolds won three People's Choice Awards over 10 years.

The Michael J. Fox Foundation works to fight Parkinson's disease. Reynolds is on the board of directors.

Reynolds wanted to help others. In 2008, he ran in the New York City Marathon. He raised more than $100,000. The money went to research for Parkinson's disease. Reynolds's dad had died from the disease. In 2023, Reynolds donated $1 million to help children in Israel and Gaza.

FOR THE PLANET

Reynolds wants to help the environment. In 2011, he produced *The Whale*. The film is a nature documentary. It is about a young killer whale.

Reynolds co-owns Wrexham A.F.C. with Rob McElhenney (right).

In 2020, Reynolds started a new project. He bought a soccer team in Wales. Wrexham A.F.C. was struggling in its league. Reynolds wanted to help the team win. He also produced *Welcome to Wrexham*. The reality series follows the team.

FOOTBALL LEVELS

In the United Kingdom, soccer is called football. The country has several different leagues. Teams that do well can move up to new leagues. The bottom teams in each league move down. Wrexham fell to the National League in 2008. That is fifth from the top. But in 2023, the team moved up a league.

Reynolds is also known for talking about mental health. He describes his struggles with anxiety. And he encourages people to get help. In 2023, he received an important award. It was the Robin Williams Legacy of Laughter Award. It came from a group that works to help people with their mental health. Reynolds hopes to make people's lives better.

In 2016, Reynolds got a star on the Hollywood Walk of Fame.

FAST FACTS

Full name: Ryan Rodney Reynolds

Birth date: October 23, 1976

Birthplace: Vancouver, British Columbia, Canada

TIMELINE

1976 — Ryan Reynolds is born on October 23 in Vancouver, British Columbia, Canada.

1991–93 — Ryan plays Billy on *Fifteen*.

1998–2001 — Reynolds plays his breakout role on *Two Guys, a Girl, and a Pizza Place*.

2012 — Reynolds marries actress Blake Lively.

2016 — Reynolds stars in *Deadpool*.

2020 — Reynolds buys Wrexham A.F.C.

2022 — Reynolds wins a People's Choice Award for being an icon.

COMPREHENSION QUESTIONS

Write your answers on a separate piece of paper.

1. Write a few sentences explaining why Ryan Reynolds wanted to play Deadpool.

2. What fact about Ryan Reynolds did you find the most interesting? Why?

3. What sitcom did Reynolds work on for four years?

    A. *Buried*

    B. *Sabrina the Teenage Witch*

    C. *Two Guys, a Girl, and a Pizza Place*

4. While filming *Buried*, Reynolds overcame his fear of tight spaces. Why might that have happened?

    A. He got to avoid his fear.

    B. He got lots of practice being in a tight space.

    C. He had to pretend to be afraid.

5. What does **script** mean in this book?

*In improv, there is no **script**. Actors make up the words as they go. They make up the story.*

    A. camera used for filming movies

    B. costume that actors wear in a play

    C. written lines that actors must learn

6. What does **frustrated** mean in this book?

*But his acting career was not taking off. Reynolds was **frustrated**. He quit acting.*

    A. excited

    B. upset

    C. happy

Answer key on page 64.

GLOSSARY

antihero
A character who doesn't act like a typical hero.

breakout
When something helps a person become very successful.

critics
People who judge works of art such as movies and music.

director
A person who leads the making of a movie.

documentary
A film or TV show that presents facts about real events.

icon
A person who is widely loved, respected, and influential.

producers
People who help plan the making of movies or TV shows.

romcoms
Short for "romantic comedies." Romcoms are funny movies about people falling in love.

sitcom
A TV show about a set of characters facing different funny events.

test footage
Scenes recorded on film to see if an idea works.

TO LEARN MORE

BOOKS

Burling, Alexis. *Hollywood*. Minneapolis: Abdo
Publishing, 2020.

Huddleston, Emma. *Chadwick Boseman*. Mendota
Heights, MN: Focus Readers, 2021.

London, Martha. *Chris Hemsworth*. Mendota
Heights, MN: Focus Readers, 2021.

ONLINE RESOURCES

Visit **www.apexeditions.com** to find links and
resources related to this title.

ABOUT THE AUTHOR

Sharon Dalgleish lives in Sydney, Australia, with her
part–Blue Heeler rescue dog. She is the author of
more than 50 books for children. She has never met
Ryan Reynolds. But she would like to!

INDEX

ANSWER KEY:
1. Answers will vary; 2. Answers will vary; 3. C; 4. B; 5. C; 6. B